HELPING THE LARGEST LIVING GENERATION FIND THEIR PLACE

MILLENNIALS
CALLING

PAUL SOHN AND DEREK BELL
FOREWORD BY TODD WILSON

A MADE FOR MORE RESOURCE

FOREWORD

Millennials Calling is the first eBook to be released jointly by Exponential, Leadership Network, and the new ministry, Made for More. I believe this is one of the most important books we've had the privilege of stewarding. The idea of helping the largest living generation find their unique place is vitally important to the future of the church, if we approach it the right way and with the right motives.

At Exponential, we've seen the vital importance and need to elevate the conversation around calling among members of the body of Christ. Our vision is that the new Made for More ministry and its resources will help inspire, encourage, and equip church leaders to see the unique giftings and callings of God's people differently.

Instead of a volunteer-centric, "we can do it, you can help" approach to mobilization, Millennials are looking for a missionary-centric, "you can do it, how can we help" approach from the church. Millennials are sensitive to being manipulated as pawns by the institutional machine. Instead of feeling used, they want to be valued for their unique contribution and role. Previous generations need to celebrate and embrace this amazing opportunity to equip the next generation to find their unique place. That's where this new book *Millennials Calling* fits so nicely.

So where did we start? By finding the right leaders to speak into this important topic. God put Paul Sohn and Derek Bell directly in our path.

Paul Sohn is a young leader truly making a difference among his Millennial peers. He started QARA, a dynamic organization to help Millennials discover their true identity and calling—to become empowered to live every day to the fullest. Paul is also the author of *Quarter-Life Calling: Pursuing Your God-Given Purpose in Your Twenties*.

Derek Bell and I had the privilege of serving Bob Buford together for almost ten years. In that decade, I had the great opportunity to witness Derek's passion for equipping men and women to walk into their Ephesians 2:10 calling. His passion and gifting are so aligned with the Made for More vision that we tapped Derek to help us launch the organization and serve as Executive Director of Made for More.

Throughout the pages of *Millennials Calling*, Paul and Derek speak from experience and great passion. Their ideas are simple yet profound. I hope you'll process these ideas both prayerfully and strategically as a means to helping the largest living generation become more effective disciple-makers as they live within the sweet spot of their unique personal calling.

Todd Wilson
CEO, Exponential
Co-founder, Made for More
Co-founder, The Buford Library

ACKNOWLEDGMENTS

If I (Derek) have done anything good for the Kingdom, it is because of the love and discipleship of my Mom and Dad and the partnership in marriage and ministry of Jennifer, my wife. Thank you to Macy, Parker and Grayson for being my three favorite people on the planet.

When it comes to walking into calling, two men who are both in the presence of their Savior shaped me greatly--Bob Buford and Greg Murtha. Bob and Greg finished well as good and faithful servants. Thank you for doing life with me. I look forward to being back alongside you again someday.

I (Paul) am deeply indebted to my mom and dad who have been instrumental in helping live out my calling. Without their ceaseless prayer, unwavering support, and godly wisdom, I would not be who I am today. Their lives are a perfect reminder that living out one's calling starts and ends with an intimate relationship with the Caller.

QARA

WE GUIDE EMERGING ADULTS TO CONNECT THEIR
CALLING TO CAREER

Your twenties is the most transformative period of your life.
This decade has the power to shape your path and propel you into
a life of significance.

Yet so many twenty-somethings feel lost. Confused. Anxious.
Disappointed.

Do you ever feel paralyzed by indecision? Have you ever felt insecure while
scrolling through your Instagram feed? You are not alone.

At QARA, we believe when you discover your true identity and calling,
you will be empowered to live every day to the fullest. QARA exists to equip,
inspire, and empower twenty-somethings to discover their True North.

As an online community and resource hub, we help you become the best
version God created you to be – fully empowered to pursue your calling and
to make a lasting impact on your family, your organization, your community
and the world.

What We offer

WORKSHOPS
Calling, Identity, Faith and Work,
Equipping Leaders of Millennials

ONLINE COURSES
How to Find Your Calling and Vocational Sweetspot in Your 20s

CAREER ASSESSMENTS
MBTI, StrengthFinder 2.0, DiSC, Career Direct

COACHING
Career Coaching, Leadership Coaching, Life Coaching

QARA
www.qara.org

Featured Made for More Resources

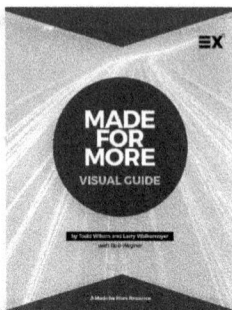

MADE FOR MORE VISUAL GUIDE

This "read in an hour," visually engaging, resource introduces and integrates three new frameworks to help shift your ministry from a volunteer based *"we can do it, you can help"* approach to a *"you can do it, we can help"* missionary focused approach.

MORE

BE-DO-GO Framework

Who am I created to BE?
What am I made to DO?
Where am I to GO?

MADE FOR MORE BIBLE STUDY

The Six Shifts of Mobilization Framework

Bible study for staff & elders that highlights six key shifts that are necessary to create a healthy culture of mobilization.

THE MOBILIZATION FLYWHEEL

Church - Missionaries - Gathering Framework

Every person needs a healthy, biblical church family. Every believer is called and empowered to be an "everyday missionary." Gatherings can become new churches, strengthen existing churches or multiply themselves.

FREE downloads at exponential.org/ebooks.

ADDITIONAL MADE FOR MORE RESOURCES

Exponential and Made for More put together a large library of FREE Resources to go along with the 2019 theme Made for More: Mobilizing God's People, God's Way.

Additional Made for More Resources

- ebooks
  - *Made for More Bible Study*
  - *Made for More Devotional*
  - *Made for More Visual Guide*
  - *Millennials Calling*
  - *The Flywheel of Mobilization*
  - *Church Different*
  - More eBooks Coming!

- Made for More Resource Kits
  - Made for More Staff and Leadership Resource Kit
  - Made for More Personal Calling Kit

- Made for More On-Line Course

- Articles & Blog Posts (A collection of blog posts on Mobilizing God's People, God's Way.)

- Video Training (An exclusive video teaching series on how you can help mobilize every Christian into their calling to make disciples where they live, work, learn and play.)

- Audio Podcasts (a series of compelling conversations with some of today's most trusted voices on their personal calling.)

- Made for More Assessment Tool (coming soon!)

For information about the 2019 Made for More theme and other FREE Made for More Resources, please visit our Made for More Resource Page: https://exponential.org/made-for-more-resources/.

INSIDE

INTRODUCTION

A tidal wave of epic proportions.

We believe that's the great opportunity we could witness if today's Millennial generation discovered and engaged in their Kingdom calling.

And we have the numbers to back up our vision.

According to the Pew Research Center, the Millennial generation (roughly born between 1980 and 2000) will be the largest living generation in the United States in 2019. Research indicates Millennials and Baby Boomers will cross paths in population numbers somewhere between 72 million and 73 million, making it the most influential living generation in the word. Millennials represent 80 million strong. By 2020, they will take over 75 percent of the workforce.[1]

And their influence goes beyond sheer numbers. Consider this. In 2013, U.S. Millennials spent $1.3 trillion and will spend more than any other generation by 2017 as they continue to enter the beginning and middle stages of their earning years.[2.]

A God-Breathed Vision

Since the launch of my book *Quarter-Life Calling*,[3] I (Paul) have had the opportunity to give hundreds of talks to Millennials, spanning from Asia to Central and North America. During my countless coaching and dialogue with Millennials, one unanswered, deep-seated question always came up: *Why am I here?*

Mark Twain is correct: "The two most important days in your life are the day you are born and the day you find out why."

The latter part of that statement has become the centerpiece of my (Paul's) life calling. That is, to help others discover their *why* through their calling.

I have witnessed the potency of the lives of Millennials who have embraced their calling. In a world where many suffer from Obsessive Comparison Disorder (OCD), Fear of Missing Out (FOMO), anxiety, panic attacks and depression, Millennials who have established a clear understanding of who they are and what they are called to do appear uncannily countercultural and different. They seem to have an overwhelmingly high sense of confidence, self-esteem, joy and peace in their lives. They truly seem to be living in their sweet spot.

God ignited a vision in my life. I wondered what would happen if:

More Millennials could discover their true identity in Christ?

More Millennials stopped comparing themselves to others and embraced their God-given identity?

More Millennials redefine their standards of success from one that is of the world to one that of the Kingdom?

More Millennials relentlessly lived out their calling?

I'm convinced the world would be a different place.

That vision for what would happen if these "wonderings" became reality compelled me to partner with Derek Bell on this book. As Derek shares below, we both felt the need to offer a unique resource for reaching and coaching this generation with so much world-changing potential.

A Picture of Future Impact

For me (Derek), one of the strangest vocational gifts God gave me was that of geography. When I joined the staff of a large church south of Nashville, Tennessee, as a community group pastor, I inherited the leadership of groups who met throughout the large Nashville area, including the city's many colleges and universities.

Based on demographics, many of my leaders were Millennials (the other three regions were dominated by Baby Boomers). I was responsible for putting groups together; making sure everyone was connected; and influencing curriculum. But as it turned out, I was really there to be a disciple maker. The way our church was set up, community group leaders were the chief disciplers--effectively making me the disciple maker.

During this time of discipling Millennials, I fell in love with the generation. Of course, I also worked with members of older generations who were outstanding. But it was the Millennials who brought a different level to their leadership and creativity--helping those they led fully embrace the life of a believer. Once they understood what we were asking of them, they were off to the races only looking back at me for subtle affirmation and encouragement.

While I was there--and later after having launched a ministry geared to helping Millennials find their place--I, like Paul, began to imagine how Jesus would be taken into every nook and cranny of society by millions of men and women who understood the unique contribution they had to offer in the advancement of the gospel.

We both see the future impact of this generation. That's why we're bringing together our experience and passion for Millennials in what we believe is a book for church and ministry leaders who are also passionate about seeing this generation reach their full potential but realize you're swimming in deep, unknown waters.

If you serve as a Christ-centered leader who desires to truly understand and impact the Millennial generation, this book will equip you with key notions of calling and practical applications of ideas and tools to enable Millennials to live out their calling.

Calling vs. Guidance

To make sure we're on the same page about the idea of calling, in this book we're using a thought from best-selling author Os Guinness, author of *The Call*. The way in which Guinness compares and contrasts "guidance" and "calling" sheds light on the calling, or purpose, we're writing about in this book.

Specifically, he writes: *"'Guidance' and 'calling' certainly overlap, but guidance is generally specific. God tells us to 'do this,' 'go there,' 'don't do this,' 'don't go there'— through the Bible and the Holy Spirit. But calling is generally entrepreneurial. In most areas of life, we do not hear God's voice or see any vision from God. Like the servants in the parable of the talents, we go about the Master's business, seeking to multiply and maximize the talents he has entrusted to us."*[4]

It is the unique calling that Os Guinness writes about that compels us to lead individual Millennials more effectively so that our churches, and big "C" Church will be different--more readient and fruitful in a world so desperate for help. In the Millennial generation, church leaders have an unprecedented opportunity to be part of a world-changing movement, but our scorecard must change.

We get in trouble when we view this opportunity through the prism of a church growth strategy—although an intentional effort to reach this generation will likely lead to church growth.

When we start to understand Millennials and their natural tendencies, help them find and pursue both their primary and personal callings, and then release them to run—these Christ followers will take Jesus with them. They *will* build the church, and they *won't* stop with our little kingdoms.

In this book, you'll find five key points from two guys—one of which is squarely a Millennial and built a ministry around working with them (Paul); the other, a pastor, who has worked with many Millennials and has the gift of perspective (Derek). Our five key points include:

1. **Calling in context.** *Conversations of calling must come in the context of discipleship.*

2. **Getting perspective.** *The more we understand about the Millennial generation, the more we understand the individuals and the potential God has placed right in front of us.*

3. **Discovering identity.** *In an age of shifting identities, knowing one's identity in Christ is a necessity.*

4. **The Millennial opportunity.** *When leaders understand the heart of the opportunity, we can prioritize our ministry.*

5. **Coaching ideas.** *We offer three lessons we have learned along the way, as well as some practical exercises you can use to help Millennials think through calling and how it plays out in their lives.*

We're discussing these ideas over the next five chapters in hopes you'll see the importance of helping Millennials find their places in God's mission—and make this an ongoing conversation in your church or ministry.

If it's already a discussion, we hope you'll take a deeper dive. We have placed links throughout the pages to "hear" your feedback. Establishing a new scorecard requires dialogue that challenges each other.

Whether you serve as a pastor, manager, non-profit leader, or Fortune 500 executive with a staff of Millennials, our hope is that this book helps you will glean important notions of calling and how to practically coach, engage, and lead Millennials to discover and live out their Kingdom calling.

Let's start this world-changing conversation!

COMMUNITY DISCUSSION (www.millennialscalling.com/community):

- How do you define "calling"?

- What excites you about helping Millennials find their place?

- How do you think the Millennial generation will impact the world?

CHAPTER 1

CALLING IN CONTEXT

Building a Foundation of Discipleship

DON'T START HERE! While this may be a good place to begin this book, it's not really a great point to start helping Millennials engage their calling. We firmly believe and have seen that any discussion on calling must take place in the larger context of discipleship.

In fact, if you tried to sketch out a linear progression of Jesus' disciples' journey from their first encounter with Jesus to their death/martyrdom, calling comes into play at the point there is some spiritual maturity.

The disciples clearly didn't understand what Jesus was calling them to do with their lives until after His death. They spent time confused, questioning Jesus, denying Jesus and squabbling. At some point in their maturation process, it clicked. They still swayed off the path from time to time, but as they continued to surrender, they marched on toward the accomplishment of their calling.

Or, it may be that the search for one's calling (many call it "purpose") is exactly what God uses to prepare someone's heart to enter into a relationship with Christ. Our experience has shown us that *wherever* an individual of any age begins their journey to discover, engage and live out their primary and secondary callings, they must be surrounded by discipleship.

This is a cornerstone understanding that's essential to helping guide Millennials in their calling journey. In any case, whether calling comes later in the maturation process, or God uses calling to get a hold of our lives, we can always work to "multiply while maturing."

A good friend recently shared that valuable idea with me. We all need a level of maturity so that we don't do harm while at the same time releasing hungry disciples to get busy doing God's work. As a discipler, I know that if I am walking in this tension, I am doing my job--it's a good tension.

Let's look at the two callings and a unique framework for both.

Our Primary and Unique Callings

In his research for his book, *More: Find Your Personal Calling and Live Life to the Fullest Measure*, author Todd Wilson found that we all have a two-part calling: a general or primary calling common to all disciples; and a personal or secondary calling that's unique to each of us.[5]

We all share the same primary or general calling as His Church—to be disciples who make disciples wherever we are and wherever we go. Scripture tells us our primary calling is to be disciples who carry the fullness of Jesus into every crack and cranny of society. Matthew's gospel gives us the Great Commission: "Therefore go and make disciples of all nations, baptising them in the name of the Father and of the Son and of the Holy Spirit."

Disciples being made in all nations is God's plan A. In Ephesians 1:22-23, Paul paints a picture of what happens when that plan is being rolled out … the fullness of Jesus fills everything: "And God placed all things under his feet and appointed him to be head over everything for the church, which is his body, the fullness of him who fills everything in every way."

Each of us also has a secondary calling but unlike our primary calling, our secondary or personal calling is unique to each one of us. Wilson describes our primary and personal callings:

> "Our general or primary calling is to be disciples who make disciples where we are! This element of calling is the fullness of Jesus flowing in us and through us to others.

> "When the Bible refers to "calling," it is most often this primary or general calling. Our general calling is common to that of all Followers of Jesus Christ."[6]

The personal or unique calling, Wilson writes, "equips us to play a unique part in accomplishing God's mission in our community.[7]

When discipling Millennials in the area of calling, this idea of two different types of calling is extremely valuable. We are all part of the Body of Christ, a family. God has designed each member of His family with a set of common expectations laid out in the New Testament.

Common to all believers is the command to make disciples, take care of orphans and widows, forgive those that have sinned against you, etc. As a part of a local body of believers, whatever that expression looks like, we all have a part to play in simply helping that family function and thrive.

Sometimes the local body needs us to rock babies, lead small groups, park cars and other activities that don't necessarily light our fires but are necessary for the benefit of the whole.

Sometimes these opportunities align with our unique calling, but most of these opportunities to serve fall under the umbrella of volunteerism. Again, we all need to volunteer. We all need to pull our weight in the family of God.

But … and this is a big but. Leaders, if you start and end the conversation around calling with volunteerism, or common calling, you are doing a disservice to those you are discipling and to the

Kingdom of God. As Millennials are actively working to feel secure in their unique reason for being, they need to experience Ephesians 2:10 happening in their lives:

> *"For we are his workmanship, created in Christ Jesus for good works, which God prepared beforehand, that we should walk in them"* (Eph. 2:10, ESV).

The very notion of "workmanship" connotes notions of being "unique" and "special," designed by the master craftsman. The word "beforehand" tells us that God has prepared these works since the beginning of time and eternity. God has been actively preparing the unique "good works" for his Millennial masterpieces to "walk" into.

This is a generation that needs to experience the alignment between who they are, who they were created to be, and what their Creator designed them to do.

Gordon Smith, president of Ambrose University writes in *Courage and Calling*:

"First, there is the call to be a Christian ... Second, for each individual there is a specific call— a defining purpose or mission, a reason for being. Every individual is called of God to respond through service in the world. Each person has a unique calling in this second sense. We cannot understand this second meaning of call except in the light of the first.[8]

Be-Do-Go

We can understand how these callings play out in our lives with what Wilson calls the Be-Do-Go framework:

- who are you created to BE

- what are you uniquely made to DO

- where you fit and GO.

Our secondary calling is our unique Ephesians 2:10 distinctive that makes each individual different and gives each of us a unique role in God's bigger plan.

In my (Derek) experience, the very revelation of this common and unique calling is freedom- producing. The idea of common calling allows me to relax into volunteer positions even when they aren't exhilarating. At the same time, the idea of having a unique calling keeps me searching the heart of God and exploring the depths of my of own soul. Then, I have an explanation for when I get that feeling that I am putting my all into a work that was … prepared beforehand … since the beginning of time.

That search offers an explanation for when I sense that I'm putting my all into a work that was ... prepared beforehand for me ... since the beginning of time. As leaders, it's up to to share this freeing truth with Millennials. This is a generation that needs to experience the alignment between who they are, what they were created to do, and where they belong.

When Millennials Skip Over Their Primary Calling

Years ago, author, entrepreneur and philanthropist Bob Buford told his Bob, Inc. team (what he lovingly called his small group of advisors, including Doug Slaybaugh, Todd Wilson and me) about a conversation he once had with Pastor Rick Warren. The details of the conversation are lost in time, but the principle of the idea is timeless.

In the early days of Saddleback Church, Pastor Rick, Buford and Bob's mentor Peter Drucker (a.k.a. the father of modern management) talked about the baseball diamond model that Rick was working out in real time.

Rick laid out the discipleship progression most people follow, going from "knowing Christ" to "growing in Christ" to "serving Christ" to "sharing Christ." Home plate to first base. First to second. Second to third and third to home.

As Rick was unpacking the model in this conversation with Bob and Peter, one of them (we don't know which) made the insightful observation that while most individuals take the typical discipleship path, some (and I believe many Millennials) will encounter Christ first through a sense of calling, or service to others.

An encounter with the Living God is exactly what we pray for, but when this happens outside of the normal maturation process inherent in discipleship, we as leaders need to begin to fill in the gaps for Millennials. While they often gravitate toward the "go" that Wilson talks about in his book, *More*, it's our job to help this generation fully embrace the "be" and the "do," as well.

In the Millennials that I (Derek) have discipled, God has used that natural pull to "do" and "go" to create space for a relationship with Him. However, it is vitally important to go back and build a strong foundation.

In my experience, their sense of calling also changes once they have a more complete understanding that comes with foundational discipleship. It is always a beautiful thing when as a discipler, you see a Millennial walk into their unique calling *and* also surrender to God's lordship.

Once that surrender comes and you see it transform their life and the way in which they live out God's calling--it becomes more about Him and His unfolding story and less about them and their activity.

The point these three giants talked about that day was the idea that in today's world, the idea of calling (by no means is it a new idea—God called Adam and Eve) is so powerful that many will feel the tug of God's calling on their life—a pull that gradually leads them back to the basics and ultimately to fully realized spiritual maturity.

Without discipleship or primary calling, however, calling becomes something else. We have all seen examples of calling when it takes place in the absence of discipleship (though you may not have known that was what was happening or how to articulate it).

Both of us have seen what happens when people pursue their unique/secondary calling without pursuing God's primary calling to make disciples.

Years ago, I (Derek) learned a valuable lesson from a friend who walked uber-high capacity men and women through the discovery process of their calling. I remember the epiphany my friend had when he began to understand that the individuals he was guiding were simply conquering the next hill and referring to it as calling.

These young men and women were certainly making incredible contributions to the Kingdom through their work, but it was an activity, not necessarily part of their spiritual journey. This particular leader was witnessing firsthand how a new believer goes around the base path the opposite way.

My friend began to lead his colleagues to actually take a step back and make sure any talk of personal calling was surrounded by ongoing discipleship and disciple making—being disciples who make disciples wherever they are.

For those individuals not willing to go back and align their personal calling with their primary calling (being discipled and being a disciple maker), my friend began to see men and women make decisions, not understanding the theological implications.

Many burned out quickly because the foundation supporting their journey was not strong enough to carry the load farther on down the road.

I (Derek) often think about a very successful business leader I knew. He was passionately captured by needs in Rwanda. Acting on that passion. this business leader attacked some educational issues in the country, bringing his connections and resources to the table.

In the early days of the ministry, his scorecard looked pretty similar to his business scorecard--revenue up and to the right, expenses down, diplomas gained, etc. But once I guided this leader to circle back and build a strong discipleship foundation, his metrics began to change.

They included more Kingdom-advancing measurements like transformed lives, students embracing their calling, etc. As this leader's life was transformed, so was the unique work to which that God had called him. It was years after he began building this foundation that I saw his journey move from success to significance and finally to surrender.

This man had the right personality and was a get-it-done type of leader. He could pretty much drive success on his own. As he grew as a disciple of Christ, he began to experience new Kingdom significance. He began to see men and women engage Jesus, as well as great education.

As the journey moved forward, you saw him surrender to the lordship of Christ. His ministry really took on a new life because it was transformed from his next hill to conquer to God's call on his life.

Social Justice Outside of Discipleship

When Millennials don't keep their personal calling in context by aligning their secondary calling with their primary calling, we can confidently say that this generation that has so much world-changing potential will stumble on all of these obstacles— especially the social justice issue.

The pull on Christ followers to join the ranks of social justice warriors is scary when they pursue that justice outside of their primary calling of being and making disciples. Should we be warriors for justice? Yes. Our faith demands that we always seek justice, but justice must be rooted in the truths of Scripture, or it quickly becomes misguided.

If you don't know by now, we'll tell you that the Millennial generation is predisposed to look for justice. But without the discipleship piece in place and with the world whispering (or yelling) in both ears, they will easily make their calling about the next ministry fad, the next activist push, or even more harmful—a well-intentioned movement that ultimately does more harm than help because it fails to understand the basic tenets of our faith and how they fit together systemically to form a consistent theology.

It seems the "love wins" movement launched years ago by some popular authors has caused a great deal of confusion. Any semi-mature disciple understands the importance of love--it is God's chief posture toward His children. Love cannot be overvalued or over-practiced.

However, when love is taken out of the context of justice, mercy, truth and other tenets of our faith, it produces an incomplete system of theology. That,in turn, produces incomplete or skewed Christian practices.

Without well-shaped orthodoxy, our orthopraxy is confused, which leads to actions and activities that don't line up with Scripture. Millennials must have well-shaped doctrinal and theological constructs to ensure their lives reflect the Truth and their calling is built on a strong foundation.

The conversation about calling must be elevated within our churches and ministries but only in the context of robust discipleship. We both are grateful for the work of discipleship. org as they continue to raise the flag of discipleship. Their model and resources are equipping all of us for the more comprehensive journey.

The organization Made for More (www.personalcalling.org) was recently launched anchored by the belief that calling is such a unique and vast aspect of discipleship.

Both organizations, along with their parent ministry, Exponential (exponential.org), are working hand-in-hand to encourage, inspire and equip the Church to help men and women of all ages discover their secondary calling and align it with their primary calling to be and make disciples.

As you understand that the calling conversation must take place in the context of discipleship, we can now work toward greater effectiveness by understanding these individuals that make up the largest living generation.

COMMUNITY DISCUSSION (www.millennialscalling.com/ community):

- Do you know of or use any frameworks for leading Millennials into their calling?

- Have you ever experienced calling-gone-wrong outside of the discipleship journey? What harm was caused?

CHAPTER 2

GETTING PERSPECTIVE

Understanding the Largest Living Generation

We're not telling you anything new when we say that perspective is important. When it comes to challenging and equipping the Millennial generation to engage their calling in the context of discipleship (pursuing both their primary calling and their secondary calling), perspective is critical.

Understanding who Millennials are and what has shaped them leads to more effective ministry. There is so much information and statistics out there about this generation. For this book, we worked to distill and share some thoughts that impact Millennials' journeys to finding their unique contribution in God's Kingdom.

For starters, the majority of Millennials don't think the Church is relevant. According to Barna Research studies that surveyed Millennials, the two most frequent words they used to describe Christianity were "irrelevant" and "extreme."[9]

In their groundbreaking book, *Souls in Transition,* sociological expert and director of the Center for the Study of Religion and Society Christian Smith and Patricia Snell say that religion is just "in the background" for Millennials.[10]

During their childhood, their local church might have been a place where they learned right and wrong. But now that they've learned it, Millennials have less need for church. Rather, many are distracted in this "in-between" transitory season when they're emerging into adulthood and sorting through all kinds of choices they must make to create their identity.

Author, pastor and researcher Ed Stetzer has noted that only one in six unchurched Millennials wanting spiritual guidance said they would look for it in a church. Even more troubling, Stetzer discovered that nine out of ten unchurched Millennials believe they can have a good relationship with God or learn how to be a Christian without the presence of church.[11]

There are multiple reasons why Millennials are less interested in the Church. Let's look at three spheres of life contributing to this disturbing reality:

Home: A large number of Christian parents have done a poor job of modeling their faith and raising their children in the Word of God. They have failed to help the next generation see Christianity in a holistic and meaningful way. The truth is before the mass exodus of Millennials from church, there was a mass exodus of fathers and mothers leaving their family. Before Millennials stopped participating in church, their parents stopped putting church as their top priority. Before the doubts got the best of Millennials, fear and doubt were already ingrained in their parents' lives.

- Many Millennials were brought up in a legalistic family.

- Many of the problems Millennials deal with stem from their parents: divorce, hypocrisy, dysfunctional relationships, legalism, overprotective parenting.

The painful reality is that the transfer of Christian faith from one generation to the next is almost non-existent. A reality that leads to profound regret. We have both heard Christians parents make comments to the effect of, "Every time we see our daughter fail, it reminds us of how we failed her." Our guess is you have heard similar comments.

According to Christian Smith, "Parents for whom religious faith is quite important are thus likely to be raising teenagers for whom faith is quite important, while parents whose faith is not important are likely to be raising teenagers for whom faith is also not important. The fit is not perfect. None of this is guaranteed or determined, and sometimes, in specific instances, things turn out otherwise. But the overall positive association is clean."[12]

Recent research backs up Smith's premise. A National Study of Youth and Religion study found that of parents who report that their faith is extremely important in their daily lives, 67 percent of their teens say faith is extremely or very important in their daily lives; only 8 percent of those parents' teens report that faith is not very, or not important in their lives.[13]

Culture: Christianity isn't portrayed well in the media. It isn't politically correct to be a Christian anymore. In today's culture, it's more socially acceptable to embrace non-Christian identities and lifestyles that stand in conflict with a biblical worldview.

Church: Over the last six decades, the American Church has more commonly been known for what it stands against rather than what it stands for. The general culture sees the church as a negative rather than as what Jesus described as a "shining city on a hill" (Matt. 5:14). Millennials are particularly perceptive. Look at the statistics:

- More than one-third of Millennials say their negative perceptions are a result of moral failures in church leadership (35 percent). Substantial majorities of Millennials who aren't part of a local church say they see Christians as judgmental (87 percent), hypocritical (85 percent), anti-homosexual (91 percent) and insensitive to others (70 percent).[14]

- Most worrisome are the two-thirds of Millennials who believe American churchgoers are a lot or somewhat hypocritical (66 percent).[15] To a generation that prides itself on the ability to smell a fake a mile away, hypocrisy is the mother of all indictments.

What Factors Have Shaped Millennials?

The following four primary factors have significantly shaped Millennials.

Helicopter parents – Millennials became the most wanted generation. By 1990, 80 percent of all fathers were in the delivery rooms attending their children's births, up from 27 percent halfway through Gen Xers' birth years. In addition, Millennials desire their parents' involvement in their lives.

According to a study by church researcher Thom Rainer, 77 percent of Millennials seek their parents' advice periodically and regularly. Millennials believe their parents can offer sound wisdom and perspective while many Boomers knew their parents couldn't.[16]

Entitlement Culture – From participation trophies on the football field to bouquets of roses after preschool dance recitals, Millennials grew up hearing they were special and unique. In one survey, 96 percent of Millennials agreed or somewhat agreed with the statement, "I can do something great."[17] Not even one respondent disagreed strongly.

Millennials were age nine before their sports teams started keeping score because a scoreboard would make the losing team feel bad. Everyone received a trophy and participation prizes. If you're a Millennial (or the parent of one) who grew up playing sports, you know exactly what we're talking about here. Your garage is probably filled with boxes of trophies you or your child received before you/they were even ten.

Emerging adulthood –What makes Millennials unique is their life stage. Emerging adulthood is a new life strategy between adolescence and full-fledged adulthood, so anywhere between eighteen to thirty years of age. Just fifty years ago, you became an adult in your early twenties. Most people graduated from high school, secured a job, became financially independent, got married and had kids all before the age of twenty-five.

Now, Millennials lag behind on traditional markers of adulthood. Being a twenty-something today is a completely different experience. For example, Millennials are entering into the fourth Industrial Revolution where the only constant is change. Seventy to eighty percent of jobs will disappear in the next twenty years. Also, the instability of the job market resulted in 20-somethings pursuing grad schools to stay competitive.

This generation has become the most educated generation. College is the new high school, and grad school is the new college. With the average student loan debt being more than $30,000, a lot of emerging adults are moving back in with their parents, delaying marriage and even switching jobs.

In 2017, about 31 percent of young adults were living back in their mom and dad's house, according to a new study from CoStar Group.[18] Consider this: an average 20-something will have seven jobs *just in their twenties.*

Ubiquitous technology – Millennials are considered "digital natives," surrounded by technology. They spend more than fifty-three hours a week with media because they use more than one kind at the same time. Computers were like toys for Millennials growing up. Now, smartphones are like a bodily appendage. McCann Worldgroup, a leading global marketing services company, reports that half of Millennials would give up their sense of smell to keep their computer or mobile phones.[19]

How Has the Church Shaped Millennials?

What we see and witness firsthand in the past always shapes who we are today—both as individuals and as generations. The sexual revolution changed how the Boomer generation thought, talked and lived. In the same way, the collapse of the American family has made Generation X'ers and Millennials hesitant to commit to relationships. We always live with the unintended consequences of those who have gone before us (as a parent, that's scary!).

Unfortunately, the Church is not immune to this phenomenon of shaping their own future ... for better or for worse. That said (just to make sure you hear it loud and clear from both of us), we love the local church and believe Jesus is choosing to use His Bride to redeem the lost.

The Church is made up of imperfect individuals, the great majority of which are doing the best they can with what they have. It's the unintended consequences of our efforts that lead to the shaping of the next generation.

For example, Millennials have watched their parents torn as they were pressured into signing up to serve in a volunteer role in church while never being asked or challenged to consider what ministry might really ignite their passion and lead to a transformed life.

If they think back, they probably saw their parents serve out of obligation with little or no "want to," or be a part of a church system that left the "real pastoring" to the paid staff. If they were lucky, their parents were able to back their way into a volunteer role that matched their church's needs but also got them closer to serving in the sweet spot of their calling.

Growing up, I (Derek), saw this play out in my own home. My dad who has always been an amazingly gifted leader was never maximized in the local churches we attended. He was a world-class salesman--working in the medical device industry. It saddens me to think of how a church could have guided my dad to really impact the Kingdom of God had they found the courage and capacity to walk him into his calling.

They never did. Instead they typically asked him to serve as an usher--he looked great in a suit and was a talented offering plate shuffler. I am sure seeing my father underutilized plays a role in my passion for seeing men and women released into their calling with their church at their back.

My fear is that for most Millennials, situations just like this turn to bitterness and rejection. Hopefully, the work of Made for More will make it normative that men like my dad are fully engaged in both their common and unique calling. He should have been an usher, but he also should have contributed so much more for the benefit of the Kingdom.

Even if they did find a role that aligned with their personal calling, so many of those volunteers had to set aside a large part of who they were to fit into the constructs of the program they were slotted into.

Unfortunately, that paradigm is alive and well today. The mobilization of disciples is one of the most significant issues the church has today. Few churches are mobilizing God's people the way He designed.

Men and women who are challenged to think creatively and strategically all day, every day, in their vocations are given a script to follow at church. Think about what happens when a willing disciple brings all of themselves to the ministry table and is then asked to stay within a small programmatic box. The church has certainly missed (and is missing) great Kingdom opportunities from men and women who are willing to give all, get creative and truly sacrifice.

A caveat: As part of a local body of believers, we all have a role to play in simply helping the body function and thrive, whatever that expression looks like. As we mentioned in chapter

1, Sometimes, the local body needs us to do activities that don't necessarily ignite or fan our passions.

Regardless of our personal calling, we all need to pull our weight in the family of God. But when we make the mistake as leaders of communicating (by our words or actions) that this service is their personal calling—that's when we have a mobilization issue.

The Impact

As observers, how has seeing this distorted view and practice of serving and mobilizing people affected Millennials?

In so many aspects of life, the Millennial generation has opted out of "catching" the Christian life from the generations before them. Many have seen the way Baby Boomers and Gen Xers are living out their lives and have decided one of two things:

- First, large portions of Millennials are deciding they want no association with our Christian faith. We have all seen the stats on how we are losing Millennials in droves, not to mention the overwhelming numbers who are never being exposed to the idea of a relationship with Christ. But we'll give you a few to drive this home: According to Barna Research, U.S. church attendance is the lowest in recent history, and most drastic among millennials:
  - Only two in ten Americans under 30 believe attending a church is important or worthwhile (an all-time low).
  - 59 percent of Millennials raised in a church have dropped out.
  - 35 percent of Millennials have an *anti-church* stance, believing the church does more harm than good.
  - Millennials are the least likely age group of anyone to attend church (by far).[20]

- Second, as Millennials are watching the faith of older generations, they are deciding they want to do it differently. They are the first generation who has options for everything. Millennials have grown up in a world with options—order your hamburger "your way"; purchase a car online with your exact specifications, etc. ... why not live out and express your faith differently?

We're excited about many of the things we're seeing from Millennials as they pursue their unique callings in the context of being and making disciples.

As Millennials create the way they live out their faith and shed some of the inauthentic and insincere practices of the older generations, it's exciting to see their creativity and the spark in the way they give their lives away, blurring the sacred and secular—never considering the idea that they should be operating within a programmatic box.

Just this week at an Exponential Learning Community in Nashville, Tennessee, we have seen Millennials who are more interested in making disciples who make disciples rather than building great cathedrals with consumer Christians.

We have seen Millennials who champion bivocational ministry so that they aren't beholden to desperate fundraising and they get to rub shoulders with others out in the marketplace. It is clear, Millennials are ready to fill new wine skins.

A Dangerous Scenario to Look Out For

A word of warning: Along with all the options available to Millennials that we have already mentioned comes the temptation to simply construct the faith and truth they want.

Constructing the way in which you live out your faith and pursue your calling is one thing. Piecemealing and customizing the truth is an altogether different scenario—one that's so dangerous and tragically, is becoming so pervasive. This is another important reason why helping any Christ follower engage their calling cannot be done outside of discipleship.

Unfortunately, we both have seen multiple thought leaders that captivate Millennial audiences who start to tweak their theology over time, often dropping foundational orthodox teaching. We can't imagine how confusing this is to men and women who don't have strong disciple makers to help them sort out some of these thoughts.

One example we see is the fragmented teaching on sin. This is not the place to get into specific theological thoughts on sin, but how incomplete is the gospel without sin creating the need for our Savior?

Collin Hansen, the editorial director of The Gospel Coalition, describes what faith looks like for millennials in the article "Our Secular Age": "There are no more singular, monolithic, obvious takes on the world. Belief has become less of an on/off switch, and more of a series of dials you can set in various degrees (post-secular, humanist, romantic, libertarian, eco-feminist, and on and on).

"So how do we set the dials today? In the Age of Authenticity (think life post-1960s), the drive is to make sure—whatever else may affect our decision—that we are 'true to ourselves.' This is how 'expressive individualism' plays a role in belief formation. Some of us may still choose traditional faiths like Roman Catholicism, evangelical Protestantism, or one of the other major world religions."

"But nobody simply inherits packages of beliefs anymore; we choose to believe (and even construct) the packages for ourselves, often as part of our self-actualization project."[21] Yes, creativity in the process of growth, and living out one's purpose is great. But as leaders, we know that truth is not created by us and thus needs no creativity. It is simply truth.

Thankfully, God baked in more creativity in the truth then we can unpack in a lifetime. In the end, our orthopraxy must follow sound biblical orthodoxy. Our responsibility is to communicate that truth to this generation and help them see the potential implications.

Pastors, a word of encouragement: The faith of Millennials will look different and sometimes *different is challenging*. When I (Derek) found myself a little agitated doing ministry with Millennials and perhaps didn't even know why, I learned to ask myself if it was because Millennials were simply doing something differently than I would.

Oftentimes, I realized that agitation just under the surface resulted from a difference in style, not substance. Then I would work to understand the differences so that I could discern whether my preferences were being stomped on; or whether I needed to guide an individual through a process of uncovering truth that needed to be addressed—a.k.a. discipleship.

So often I needed to bite my lip and simply let ministry happen in a way that would not be my preference, yet was still consistent with Scripture. I learned that as a Gen X'er, I needed to die to my way of doing things so that Millennials could lean into their design.

For example, when I led a group of leaders at our church, I noticed a difference in how Millennials and older generations led. Older leaders would make decisions in a vacuum: "We are going to meet at 6 p.m. on Sunday nights, and we are going to start by studying this curriculum."

My tendency is make the best decision with the information I have. Millennials are much more inclusive and collaborative. They always wanted to get feedback from the group. One of the many assets Millennials have is more patience to hear from everyone and give everyone a voice.

When you are working to lead people on a journey, isn't collaboration and buy-in on the front end a better leadership model? I believe it is, and it often takes a different mindset to make it work.

The Challenge of Information

Think for a minute about growing up in a world where there are no gatekeepers to information—for better or for worse. When I (Derek) was growing up, understanding how photosynthesis worked required us to hunt down a biology teacher or head to the library. Or better yet, consult the six-foot row of World Book Encyclopedias that my parents so graciously purchased for us.

But now, with the help of Siri, Google Assistant and Alexa, you don't even need to be able to type to find out about photosynthesis and so much more. You just simply ask. However, in coaching Millennials we must remember that they might have information and knowledge, but that does not always translate into wisdom.

If there are no gatekeepers to information or knowledge, Millennials often get to the answers prior to a process that leads to wisdom. As men and women coaching Millennials, we must remember that while they might have information and knowledge, that doesn't necessarily translate into wisdom.

We must help younger generations process what they have learned while applying the lens of experience in a way that increases wisdom.

COMMUNITY DISCUSSION (www.millennialscalling.com/community):

- What have you learned about Millennials that everyone should know?

- What victories or failures have you experienced while discipling Millennials in the area of their calling?

- What statistics or characterizations of Millennials seem incongruent with your experiences?

CHAPTER 3

THE MILLENNIAL OPPORTUNITY

Finding the Connection from Sunday to Monday

Millennials are not particularly gifted at one thing that has hurt generations of Christ followers: compartmentalization. Thank goodness! We may finally be seeing the end of generations that go to church on Sunday and then act completely different Monday through Saturday.

This generation doesn't want their lives to be compartmentalized. Instead, they want their faith to run seamlessly through every part of their lives--where they live, work and play.

According to a 2010 Pew Research report, only three out of ten Millennials say they are confident they have found their career. At the same time, some 70 percent of Millennials say that career is central to their identity.[22]

The vocation conversation is critical. Failure to show Millennials how their faith and work connect is a major contributor to the young adult dropout rate from church community. In David Kinnaman's watershed book, *You Lost Me*, he estimates that some 5 million young adults today leave the church or are putting their faith "on hold" in large numbers.[23]

As president of Barna Group and best-selling author of *Good Faith, You Lost Me, and unChristian,* Kinnman is recognized as one of the leading research voices identifying and studying trends in Christianity and the local church.

In *You Lost Me*, Kinnaman argues that one of the most important reasons for that "on-hold" status happening is that most churches don't provide a connection between Sunday and Monday. One of the most recurring themes in his research with Christian dropouts, he writes, is the idea that "[the Christianity they've been taught] does not have much, if anything, to say about their chosen profession or field ... It is a modern tragedy.

"Despite years of church-based experiences and countless hours of Bible-centered teaching, millions of next-generation Christians have no idea that their faith connects to their life's work."[24]

During my (Paul) first five years working in corporate America since college graduation, I rarely heard a specific teaching or sermon at church on how faith had a tangible impact on my career. So I naturally figured the church was not conducive for me to find answers to the disengagement, frustrations and interpersonal challenges I was facing at work.

The subtle impression I got from ministry leaders was rather an abstract reply: pray more, read the Bible, and God will guide you. While the pastor's advice wasn't incorrect, his good intentions failed to translate into effective outcomes regarding my work and career.

Studies show the importance of teaching theology of work, calling and vocation. Of those surveyed, 45 percent of Millennials who have remained active in the church say they learned to view their gifts and passions as part of God's calling versus 17 percent of church dropouts. In addition, 29 percent are more likely to have learned how the Bible applies to their field or career interests versus 7 percent.[25]

My friend Collin, a young business leader in Nashville's music industry, recently made a wholesale change in his life to connect some powerful dots. Collin and his wife had their first child several years ago. Soon after, he left the music industry to launch a career as a financial advisor--opening an office with a well-known firm.

As Collin researched this firm, he was attracted to their commitment and strategy to honestly help people wisely steward their resources while not being a sell-at-all-cost machine. In addition, Collin and Katie made this somewhat risky move because of the firm's family-friendly orientation.

As soon as Collin launched his new office, he also started a community of young men who have met over the course of several years to grow together as young business leaders, husbands and fathers. Collin is a great example of a Millennial who is bringing all the dots of his personal life and vocation together to form a consistent picture.

He is using his gifts of entrepreneurialism to launch different initiatives while also maximizing his ability to gather young men who, like him, desire to grow in every way during a foundational season of life.

Many church leaders would look at Collin and work to guide him into vocational ministry--he has all the right giftings. Collin knows the Word of God, is a great encourager, has a pastoral spirit ... the list goes on.

For years, he was part of a church culture that put marketplace leaders on a pedestal as ministers of the gospel out in the marketplace--out where they could engage people who need the Good News. Thankfully, he is maximizing his calling and making a tremendous difference as a Millennial hero maker.

Are You Encouraging Culture Makers or Culture Avoiders?

These 20-somethings like Collin want their marketplace vocations affirmed. But instead, they hear theologically misguided teaching that "spiritual" work is superior to "secular" labor.

They desire guidance and equipping on what it means to bring their faith to work and how to renew culture through it. Instead, inside their congregations they have faced suspicion for their choice to work in fields like science, fashion and film. Coddled by overprotective parents and churches, they also have been warned to eschew the world and deploy their artistic talents only inside the church, where things are safe.

In *You Lost Me*, Kinnaman notes that these young adults "want to be culture-makers, not culture avoiders."[26] Their churches have dismayed them with simplistic black-and-white answers that don't match the complexity they sense in their world. He quotes one 20-something young woman, Kellie, who pleads with church leaders to change:

> "I am misunderstood by my Christian community because I am young and because I am a woman. People often assume that my international development work is just a 'phase,' done for my own fulfillment, as if I do it for the thrill or for the snapshots I bring home.
>
> "I would like my community to see my work for what it really is: the best thing I can do to act out the heart of Christ. It's not a phase, but an important part of who Christ made me to be. Our work doesn't look like a traditional Christian ministry.
>
> The name of Jesus isn't in our title, and evangelism isn't the primary focus of our daily activities. But we are working for God's Kingdom, and believe this is the way God would have us reach people for His purposes. God has placed a dream and calling within us, and we ask that the church, rather than seeing us as young and idealistic, would see us as warriors of God who are acting as the arm of Christ, reaching the world with love, hope, and empowerment."[27]

3 Principles for Connecting Sunday to Monday

My (Derek) experience has taught me several principles for guiding those under my leadership to connect Sunday to Monday.

Language Matters

The first principle is built on the idea that "language matters." How you refer to yourself, your ministry, lay leaders, their ministry and everything in between matters in setting culture.

Every time you elevate how you talk about lay leaders, every time you serve them in word and deed, every time you give them credit rather than take it for yourself reinforces that leaders who spend their Monday through Saturday outside the church offices are the real heroes.

One great example of this comes out of Ethos Church in Nashville. I was recently facilitating a Learning Community cohort for Exponential. Our host church, Ethos Church in Nashville, does something I love. They call their small groups or community groups, "House Churches."

I think this language goes a long way in forming culture for Millennials or others that helps blur the lines between clergy and laity. If lay people are leading "Houses Churches" (even in the context of a larger congregation), they need to assume the responsibility of its pastor.

When Millennials see themselves as ministers of the gospel and don't depend on hired clergy, they leave Sunday and begin to act like pastors on Monday where they live, work and play.

To blur these lines while I was on church staff, I continually worked to downplay my role (not in a disrespectful way) and elevate their role and responsibility. I worked to be one of them--it just so happened that my contribution to the Kingdom was different and my paycheck came from a different place.

I felt good about empowering men and women, giving them encouragement and permission to lead others and shepherd them spiritually. This doesn't require devaluing your role as paid staff--it simply shapes how others see themselves as men and women with gospel purpose.

You can do it, how can we help?

The second principle I employed is simply letting ministry go undone. What? When you are leading a group of people, in any endeavor, they will have a plethora of ideas. In a local church setting, everyone has ideas for ways to live out the gospel.

When you are on church staff, those ideas typically come in the form of, "Why don't we do this…feed the local homeless population, throw a Christmas party at the children's home, etc. Often times, those lay leaders are really saying: ."we want you to lead the efforts to feed the local homeless population" or "we will come for the party if you do all the work to actually throw a Christmas party for the children's home—we will bring presents too." Those ministries and others are great, but what I learned to say is, "I really think you can do it, how can we help?"

My heart longs to help the kids at the children's home, and I would find myself attaching to ideas on the table (at least some of the ideas). But, I learned that I needed to be okay if I put that mantle of responsibility and leadership on the lay leader and they dropped the ball.

They weren't letting me down personally; they were just letting a ministry opportunity slip through their hands. Or, perhaps God was nudging them away from that opportunity and to another opportunity. In any case, in my role I needed to focus on their growth and maturity and let them focus on the ministry that would either get done, or not.

When I focused on the disciple-making leaders that I was discipling, more ministry got done and more growth happened in those leaders than if I was out working to accomplish every great ministry idea that came my way.

Another way to look at this principle when dealing with a little less mature disciples comes from my friend and mentor, Bob Buford. When Bob was helping someone walk into their calling or lead a group in certain direction, he would often apply his principle: "my job is to guide and direct energy, not supply it."

When I tell a Millennial, "that is a great ministry idea, how I can help?" and it becomes obvious they need a little help to get started, I then ask, "how can I guide you and help you put your energy in the right place?"—while being careful to not carry that burden for them. I learned that it helped me if I consciously thought, *where is the energy coming from to get this done – me, or them?*

Challenging to More

The third principle in helping connect Sunday to Monday is simply inspiring those you lead to accomplish something worthy of their best efforts. If you listen to what God is telling a Millennial who has a willing heart to do something for the Kingdom and inspire them to go after that wholeheartedly (even raising the bar some), Millennials will most often rise to the occasion. In my experience, if you listen well and throw out a challenge that really engages a Millennial, they will step up to the plate.

COMMUNITY DISCUSSION (www.millennialscalling.com/community):

- How have you seen Millennials effectively engage culture?

- In your ministry, how do you encourage individuals to connect Sunday to Monday?

CHAPTER 4

IDENTITY

Helping Millennials Understand Whose They Are

As I (Derek) was taking my eleven-year-old to her soccer game this weekend, the song "Who You Say I Am" by Hillsong Worship filled the car. Without hesitation, I turned my daughter's pre-game preparation into an awkward, emotional "dad-moment."

The heart of the emotion I experience when I hear that song, and those truths, is the pain and sorrow I feel for my children knowing the world is going to tell them so many lies about who they are. We know what the world is telling Millennials about their identity—I can't imagine what Gen Y'ers, like my children, will hear in the future.

Because we *all* need to be reminded from time-to-time (and remind those we lead) of our identity, let the truth behind these lyrics sink in and once again tell you that you are who He says you are. Think about these words as they relate to you and the Millennials in your path and ministry.

Who am I that the highest King
Would welcome me?
I was lost, but He brought me in
Oh His love for me
Oh His love for me

Who the Son sets free
Oh is free indeed
I'm a child of God
Yes I am

Free at last, He has ransomed me
His grace runs deep
While I was a slave to sin
Jesus died for me
Yes He died for me

Who the Son sets free
Oh is free indeed
I'm a child of God
Yes I am
In my Father's house
There's a place for me
I'm a child of God
Yes I am

I am chosen
Not forsaken
I am who You say I am
You are for me
Not against me
I am who You say I am.[28]

Millennials are growing up in a time when the world tells them they can reshape their identity into anything they so desire.

If you don't like your gender, you can reidentify. If you don't like your spouse, you can just find another you like better. If you don't want to be labeled a sinner saved by grace, you can simple reidentify out of this teaching. If you feel this way, just be this. Your identity is not set … until you feel like it is set (then you can always reset it later).

Just imagine the confusion an entire generation can experience in an age when absolutes are not consistently and effectively reinforced.

Identity and Personal Calling

What does our identity in Christ have to do with the idea and truth of personal calling? Everything! As we talked about in chapter one, our secondary calling is such a personal and distinct journey for each unique individual. Our personal calling can't be confused with our neighbor's or even your spouse's. Calling falls at the crux of knowing God and understanding yourself.

For all of us, especially Millennials, we have to know who we are before we discover what we're supposed to do and where we should be going—the BE-DO-GO framework we talked about in chapter 1. When those three parts of our calling don't align, we run the risk of losing ourselves … our identity.

For example, while we may know what we're supposed to DO, we compromise who we were designed to BE as Christ's heirs to achieve our goals.

Millennials are a generation intoxicated with "doing." As Os Guinness writes so insightfully in *The Call*, "Before you are called to do, you are called to be. Before you are called to something, you are called to someone. You cannot know what you are supposed to do until you know who you are. You can't know who you are until you know whose you are."[29]

When asked to define yourself, you may consider a list of factors: age, race, culture, gender, occupation, religion, possessions, family of origin. All these characteristics are good things, but they can become insecure foundations on which to build our identity and calling, especially for Millennials.

Instead, we must help this generation build their identity and calling on something unchangeable. As Jesus tells us (and HillSong Worship reminds us): you are a child of God. Guiding Millennials to a rock-solid understanding of their identity in Christ is of utmost importance.

It cannot be overlooked or circumvented in the discipleship journey. When our identity (our BE) and calling (our DO) align, we begin to engage in the Kingdom work God has called us towards. Consider Mark's account of Jesus' baptism:

"In those days, Jesus came from Nazareth of Galilee and was baptized by John in the Jordan. And when he came up out of the water, immediately he saw the heavens being torn open and the Spirit descending on him like a dove. And a voice came from heaven, 'You are my beloved Son; with you I am well pleased'" (Mark 1: 9-11).

Before Jesus performs any miracle, heals the sick or walks on water, He is reminded of His true identity as God's beloved Son. In other words, Jesus' identity is anchored in His relationship with His Father.

Think about that for a minute. Before Jesus does any work, the God of the universe says His Son's identity is secure. That He is good enough for who He is. Jesus doesn't have to prove Himself to "earn" love.

We have observed this as a perennial struggle among Millennials. They tend to skip over discovering their identity in Christ, choosing instead to focus on their personal calling. They intellectualize their identity as Jesus' heir in their heads, but helping them believe it in their hearts is one of the greatest challenges we've faced in working with Millennials.

Since the launch of my book *Quarter-Life Calling*, I (Paul) have had the opportunity to speak to a few thousands of

Millennials and field their honest questions about calling/vocation. Surprisingly, I learned the conversation of calling was rather premature for many of them. Somehow I presumed they knew who they were. But in many of their questions, I could sense an insecure foundation of who they were.

Many lacked confidence. Some struggled with anxiety and panic attacks. Others suffered from depression. In other words, I realized a large number of Millennials struggled to see themselves through God's eyes. The reason they were stuck on the calling question was because they had yet to answer the identity question. Your identity is simply what you believe about yourself. It's answering the question, "Who am I?" Only when Millennials defined themselves through God's eyes would they experience true freedom.

In my workshops, I began to facilitate a life map exercise, which soon became one of the foundational exercises I used to help Millennials see their life story from God's vantage point. I have received text messages, emails, and phone calls from Millennials who were elated to notice a change of perspective in how they saw themselves (we share this exercise among the the tools we provide in chapter five).

Another way I help Millennials see themselves through God's eyes is to ensure they palpably experience the love of God. Only by experiencing the love of God can you truly understand that you are a child of God. They need to understand and embrace how much God loves them.

In her book, *Without Rival*, author Lisa Bevere shares how one day she dozed off at her laptop working on her manuscript for her next book. When she woke up, she writes that she suddenly heard the Holy Spirit say, "I do not love my children equally."[30]

"But God," she told Him, "You've got to love us all the same. It's not fair."

Then she felt God tell her, "I don't. Same would mean one of you would be replaceable. Equal means love can be measured, but my love is immeasurable. I do not love my children equally. I love them uniquely."

The truth is that each and every person on this earth has been fashioned for the love of God regardless of our age or generation. Our Father's love cannot be likened to a pan of brownies that a loving parent cuts into equal portions, so that no child feels slighted. God's unconditional love for us is not subject to portion control.

Do you realize that God loved us before there was a beginning, and His love for us knows no end? We can turn from Him, run away, and even make our bed in hell, but our actions will not stop His *agape* love.

This is so critical because identity rooted in anything apart from a personal relationship with Jesus drives us away from our calling. This is especially true for Millennials. This generation is consistently tempted to prove themselves and earn God's approval through their work.

In other words, instead of being anchored with a secure sense of identity that's expressed in their vocation, they tend to define their identity in the work they do.

When considering our identity, we can go back to Ephesians 2:10. This identity-shaping verse reminds us, "*for we are His workmanship, created in Christ Jesus for good works, which God prepared ahead of time for us to do.*" We are *His* workmanship—not our own.

We have been carefully crafted by the master craftsman who always knows exactly what He's doing. As leaders, we have to affirm this generation that they are not the result of mass production with a guaranteed rate of failure or need for adjustment. Even the best assembly lines in the world produce lemons at a predictive rate.

If Millennials' identity is not rooted in and dependent on our Father, helping them find and engaging in that work He has planned for them is near impossible.

The Purpose of Identity

Millennials need to understand (and it's our responsibility to help them make the connection) that their identity is not an end in itself, but for the sake of service to the Most High King.

1 Peter 2:9-10 says, *"But you are chosen people, a royal priesthood, a holy nation, God's special possession, that you may declare the praises of him who called you out of darkness into his wonderful light."*

I (Derek) had the great privilege of walking with a young attorney years ago. This attorney and his family were a big part of our family's life, and they were well acquainted with our journey of adopting our oldest daughter.

One early morning, Joel said that he and his wife were praying about adopting a child, but he was afraid he could never love an adopted child as much as his biological daughter. We talked through his question intently. Years later, they have an amazing little boy they call son, through adoption.

Joel and his wife walked directly into their call to adopt their son, and now Joel continues to give away his life by serving on the board of Both Hands, an organization that helps families raise funds for their adoption.

Watching Joel move from concern about his heart and his capacity to love to an abounding love for his son has been one of the most rewarding parts of my journey. Joel's identity is now one of adoptive father, as well as adoption advocate who will impact many lives over many years. This speaks directly into Joel's identity as adopted child of God with a new calling prepared beforehand by His father.

God created each of us to be who we are so that we might all declare the praise and glory of who He is. He gives us our identity so that He can be seen through us. We are His image bearers. Who we are is for the sake of His glory and His Kingdom.

Understanding Our Priesthood Identity and Role

After discipling many Millennials, you begin to understand how the failure to understand some basic theological points plays into their everyday journey. One foundational teaching we have too often left out is "the priesthood of all believers" that Paul identifies and defines in Ephesians chapter four. When this vital teaching is missing from our identity as Christ followers, that gap shows up in how we live our lives.

Since the launch of the early church, the role of laity and clergy has ebbed and flowed. At times, the laity has more actively taken on "priestly" roles while at other times in our history, the clergy has grabbed the reins and run ahead.

It's hard to put yourself in a pre-Luther time when the prevailing belief said that we needed a human intercessor to approach the throne and understand Scripture for ourselves.

Imagine working to comprehend your unique role in God's Kingdom if everyone told you that you needed a chaperone to approach the Author of your purpose. You can start to see why Luther rebelled so vehemently and dramatically as he expressed the truth he read in Scripture.

Satan's brilliant scheme is to not come at us in a head-on assault like Luther fought against, but rather to come from the flanks. Think about the generations of well-intended Christ followers who have been lulled into latency by the subtle idea that, as laity, they had certain (lesser) roles and responsibilities in carrying out Kingdom work —while the licensed, ordained, seminary-graduating clergy had the more serious roles and responsibilities.

I (Derek) remember sitting at lunch with a group of business leaders walking through a gospel engagement framework (taught by IHS Global in more than one hundred countries). The framework they teach is easy, gospel-centered and designed to happen in real life (as opposed to just sounding good in theory).

After hearing the overview of this framework, a young business leader in the group stood up and said, "That sounds great, I think I could use those ideas with people, then get them to 'you pastor guys' to close the deal."

I loved that this friend was willing to be part of these gospel conversations, but it broke my heart that he only saw his role in someone's journey going only so far. He didn't understand his identity and thus, role, as a royal priest.

Living Out This Royal Role

Part of the challenge is also our success. Yes, we have moved beyond the notion that we need an intercessor to approach the throne of God in prayer or interpreting His Word. And beyond thinking that only official clergy can perform the sacraments.

However, we're missing the truth that our royal identity as part of the priesthood of believers goes further and deeper into our daily life. This is key to unleashing the latent potential of the Millennial generation.

As leaders, we have to help the Millennials in our path understand that they're not living out the pro-active, life-on-mission extension of the role as part of a royal priesthood. Timothy George, author and dean of the renowned Beeson Divinity School, expounds on this:

In other words, the priesthood of believers is not a prerogative on which we can rest; it is a commission which sends us forth into the world to exercise a priestly ministry not for ourselves, but for others—'the outsiders'—not instead of Christ, to be sure, but for the sake of Christ and at his behest.[31]

We claim the idea of us as priests for what it does for us (direct access to our Father), but we tend to leave it there, not allowing the responsibility to push us to carry the fulness of Jesus into every nook and cranny of society.

We don't take hold of every promise we've been given— that we are holy priests who happen to put food on the table as accountants, web developers, elementary teachers, etc.

When the Millennials I (Derek) have discipled started to incorporate the full idea of the priesthood of the believer into their identity, I watched how they began to fully embrace their identity and responsibility of being a minister of the gospel.

In 2009, when I joined the staff of a megachurch in Brentwood, Tennessee, I learned a valuable lesson in how culture plays into the notion of the priesthood of all believers. My position on staff was community group pastor.

We put so much emphasis on doing life in small groups that my five colleagues in similar roles turned out to be the pastors of our sub-congregations—we just never taught behind the podium. The group's other four pastors moved from different areas of the country specifically to be in this role while I transitioned in from a businessman and lay leader at the church.

We all helped adults find community groups and train leaders, but the majority of my time was spent discipling men. I knew a lot of the guys I began to disciple before joining the church staff, and some of them are my very best friends today.

After several years of doing life as a community group pastor, our team started to see how the relationship I had with the men I discipled looked different than the relationship with the guys my colleagues discipled.

Though we were doing many of the same things, our relationship just looked different. My relationship was more casual. We were invited to do life with the other families more often and were just more integrated into the community.

This even showed up in my wife's relationships. Jennifer formed deep friendships and really learned to walk alongside of the families under my care. Because of these dynamics, Jennifer and I thoroughly enjoyed ministry together at the church even though we were told that the church was hiring me and Jennifer was not expected to do ministry with me.

I certainly appreciated the sentiment that she was not expected to treat ministry as a vocation, but we sure had a good time doing ministry together.

As our group was talking about this, it dawned on me that I was treated differently because I was one of them, working in the marketplace and then given the privilege of being paid by the church to focus on them and others while setting aside other money-making endeavors. The men and women I led never saw me as hired clergy brought in to lead them.

And I worked hard to create a culture that helped people see their pastor (me) as nothing special—*they* were the heroes on the front lines of ministry. They took on the mantle of the priesthood because they knew their "pastor" was really no different than them.

I tell that story to to show you that when someone sees and understands their identity as being a minister of the gospel, it changes how they see themselves--and how they think God sees them. And it changes how they operate in His Kingdom. If we don't help Millennials understand their identity in Christ and role in Kingdom life, they will never search for their unique contribution to the Kingdom.

Feeling comfortable coaching Millennials can take practice and persistence. Hopefully, up to this point we have provided some helpful insights and thought leadership to help you shift the paradigm in your heart and head. Now we want to provide some tactical ideas for leading or coaching Millennials.

COMMUNITY DISCUSSION (www.millennialscalling.com/community):

- How do you see Millennials specifically struggle with their identity?

- What have you learned about helping Millennials solidify their identity in Christ?

- Has the idea of "the priesthood of the believer" influenced your ministry? How?

CHAPTER 5

LESSONS FROM HERO MAKERS

Discovering 3 Powerful Coaching Ideas

W e want to leave you with three powerful ideas from our coaches that have helped us shape the way we approach Millennials with the idea of calling; and then four exercises that have proven valuable in our ministries.

Idea #1: Be the catapult…

In his (with Warren Bird) seminal book, *Hero Maker*, pastor and Exponential President Dave Ferguson defines a hero maker as *a leader who shifts from being the hero of their own story to making others the hero in God's unfolding story.*[32]

One such hero maker in so many lives was and is *Halftime* author and Kingdom entrepreneur Bob Buford. About a decade before his death (April 18, 2018), Bob was given an idea that governed his work the last decade of his life. And it translates well to church leaders as we reach Millennials and help them pursue their personal calling.

As a part of Bob's own discipleship—as well as a mechanism for getting things done—was the formation of his Bob, Inc. group I (Derek) talked about earlier. Several guys gathered around Bob, learned from him, and then multiplied him. One of those guys was a retired Rear Admiral of the U.S. Navy, Ed Allen. The idea that Ed gave Bob and those around him is a huge reminder to us as leaders as we disciple Millennials. Bob shares the idea better than anyone...

I was given an exceptional image by a friend of mine, Ed Allen, a retired Navy Admiral, now working as an executive coach. He was an F-14 pilot, then a squadron leader, then the captain (CEO) of an aircraft carrier. He explained to me, "You are the **catapult**, *not the carrier."*

When I wondered out loud what he meant with this startlingly unfamiliar metaphor, Ed asked whether I had seen the movie Top Gun, *which casts Tom Cruise as a hotshot F-14 carrier-based jet jockey. Virtually everyone I know has seen that Jerry Bruckheimer film (three times for me). Ed then said, "The key to naval aviation is the catapult." If you have seen* Top Gun, *you will never forget the first scene where double-barreled jets are flung into the early morning dawn. Bring it to mind.*

Here is the way Ed explained it to me, "A fully armed F-14 is 60,000 pounds of dead weight. It needs to achieve in excess of 150 knots airspeed within the approximately 200 feet of the carrier deck. It takes around 2.3 seconds, and if you are the pilot, it's the greatest show on earth. It wouldn't happen without the catapult."

Then Ed said something that was a moment of true honest-to-goodness enlightenment for me, like a whack on the head. He said, "You are the catapult." You are not the pilot, you are not the plane, you are not the carrier or its captain, and you will never see the final result—the target. You are the force of encouragement that is needed to get the plane airborne on its mission. That's it!"

Earlier I had been told, "At this stage of your life, it is your job to release and direct energy not to supply it." ... It also clarifies what

I intend to do personally, perhaps for the rest of my life: being the catapult, not the carrier."

As leaders who are working with Millennials, it is so tempting to make ourselves into the ship, or the pilot, or the plane, or even the bombs being deployed. However, if we take on the burden of doing the ministry, we are robbing a Millennial of the joy and blessing of stepping up.

If I (Derek) make a Millennial my helper but don't give them the associated responsibility, they have no opportunity to grow. When I am working to intentionally launch a Millennial in whatever they sense God is asking of them, I literally step back from the situation and ask myself: *What part do I feel like I am playing in this scenario? How do I focus on being the catapult in this Millennial's journey?*

Idea #2: Replace Yourself

In the arena of walking individuals into their calling, I (Derek) was influenced greatly by Greg Murtha who was mentored by Bob Buford. One great idea that Greg taught me was that being afraid to replace myself would limit my ministry.

One palpable fear I dealt with in ministry (and I know others do as well) is value. I often thought, and still do, "do I offer enough value to my church, my ministry? Do I provide enough value for them to keep me around." What a hard place to be when you are working to release others into ministry but you're worried about your own value.

Greg taught me that in God's economy you always win when you promote others more than yourself and that when you brag on others more than yourself the Kingdom wins—and so do you in the end. I even watched Greg go to the extreme when he would recommend others for his job, or jobs he might be called on to fill if he thought they could be more effective for the Kingdom.

In a ministry setting, that means finding someone and heaping praise and credit on them and even giving that individual parts of your responsibility if they can do it better than you.

There are two unintended consequences to always giving others credit and actively working to replace yourself. First, unintended consequence is that people see what you are doing and also start to do it until a culture is created that simply gets things done for the Kingdom and no one is spending energy to attain credit.

The second unintended consequence is that we, as Robert Lewis teaches in Men's Fraternity, get to place expectations on God for a "greater reward." When times are more challenging, it's assuring to know that we are doing what God has asked us to do and that even we if we're not rewarded here on earth, God is storing up treasures for us to enjoy for eternity. In Bob Buford,'s words, "men, I have done the math; and eternity is longer than time."

Idea #3: The Danger of Being Prescriptive

As a younger leader, I (Derek) got myself in trouble while I worked to help Millennials engage their calling—I was being prescriptive. The Cambridge Dictionary defines prescriptive as "tending to say what someone should do or how something should be done."

As I got to know the young men in our group, I would hear about their past and their experiences and then begin to see their strengths. All the while, I was forming my own opinion of how God might use them. As the discipleship journey continued, I would start dropping hints of what I thought their calling was all about.

Keep in mind, I did this with the best of intent. After all, I was older and at least thought I was wiser.

It wasn't until one day the most effective catapult I knew, Greg Murtha (another man highly impacted by Bob Buford), sat me down and explained to me that being prescriptive hurt the process God has for these men. His words stung, but they were also eye-opening.

I started paying attention to how Greg launched people. He never said things like, "It sounds to me like you need to do this," or "Based on what I know of you, I think you need to explore this avenue."

Greg understood several things. First, people need to come to their own conclusions about something as serious as God's call in their life. When we are handed things, even ideas, we don't take full ownership. Greg witnessed people who had been "given" their calling. It seemed right at the time but quickly waned as they realized that what they had heard was from their friend, not God.

Second, Greg knew himself well enough to know that he always brought an agenda to the table—even when trying to resist. When discipling men and women, we always take into account our relationship with them; often we bring our own unarticulated selfishness to the table.

I have been in relationships when I didn't want to launch or deploy a disciple because that meant I would not get as much time with the individual as I wanted.

Admittedly, the reverse is also true. I've been in discipleship relationships where I wanted to launch (maybe a better word is "send") this guy because I wanted a good excuse to *not* have to hang out. In either case, I could steer the calling discussion based on my desires if I was being prescriptive.

As they helped individuals probe the heart of God, Greg and Bob would ask question after question. They would certainly point out observations about the individual's gifts and how they were uniquely designed. But they were never prescriptive.

It was enlightening to see men and women squirm as both leaders refused to answer the question, "So, what should I do?" Bob and Greg knew better than to give in and provide prescriptions when asking questions would more than suffice.

They had the wisdom not to short-circuit the process of an individual searching the heart of God. Instead, they knew that God's unique calling is so intimate that when we try to insert ourselves into someone else's calling, we tend to muddle things up.

In addition to these three big ideas, we have more granular ideas to help you guide the largest generation into their calling. Check out the following Appendix.

COMMUNITY DISCUSSION (www.millennialscalling.com/community):

- Has a hero maker played a role in your life and ministry?

- How do you play the role of hero maker?

- What has happened when you were prescriptive with calling in the lives of those you lead?

APPENDIX

Leaders Toolkit

Every leader needs a toolkit. Following are four practical and proven exercises you can distribute to team members who are working with Millennials and helping this generation discover their personal calling—helping them identify their BE-DO-and GO.

These exercises are designed for anyone but we have primarily used them with Millennials. Our prayer is that these helpful tools will offer resources for both you and the leaders you coach who disciple Millennials.

Exercise #1: Reflected Best Self

If we want to be objective about our strengths, we need other people to hold up the mirror. When we see our reflection through the eyes of people in our inner circle of influence, we begin to really identify an objective view of our strengths and talents.

Organizational expert and prolific author Robert Quinn and his peers created this exercise, which many business leaders and students have described as "eye-opening." Some even call it life-changing. Here are the steps (remember, these are geared to discipling Millennials):

1. **Enlist your inner circle and ask for feedback.** Identify ten to twenty people who know you well from different walks of life and ask them to write a story about a time when you were at your best. You can ask questions such as, "Tell me about a time when I excelled" or "Tell me when I was fully alive."

   When choosing your inner circle, it's best to select a diverse group of friends, family members, colleagues, and mentors who can paint a comprehensive picture of your strengths.

2. **Find common themes.** Once the feedback arrives, look for the common themes that appear in multiple stories. Make a list of the themes, the key examples that support each other, and what they suggest about your strengths.

3. **Create your self-portrait**. Summarize and distill the accumulated information. Use it to create a brief profile of who you are when you're at your best. The description should weave together themes from the feedback with your self-observation into a composite of who you are.

4. **Put your strengths into action.** Create an action plan for how and when you'll utilize your strengths. Create a specific timetable and strategy around how to make this strength come alive in different dimensions of your life.[33]

Exercise #2: Stop Doing List: 20/10 Exercise

In his best-selling book, *Good to Great*, Jim Collins suggests a powerful exercise that he uses with young leaders.

Here's the scenario: Suppose you woke up tomorrow and received two phone calls. The first phone call tells you that you have inherited $20 million, no strings attached. The second tells you that you have an incurable and terminal disease, and you have no more than ten years to live. Now, the question isn't what will I do with my life. Instead, the question becomes, "What would be on my *stop-doing* list?"[34]

Note: This tool helps Millennials focus on identifying and doing what's most important. It contrasts with the message of today's world, which screams "do more!" Sometimes streamlining and doing less will help resolve the issue.

Exercise #3: Write Your Obituary

Ask Millennials to write an obituary as a true account of their life to date. When it's ready, encourage them to look over their obituary and ask specific questions:

- If I died today, would I die satisfied?

- Am I satisfied with the direction my life is headed?

- Am I happy with the legacy I'm creating?

- What's missing from my life?

- What do I need to do for my obituary to be "complete"?

Then, have them write another obituary, listing all the things they wish they had done with their lives.

Exercise #4: Turning Back the Clock

Our lives are a story. We can discover what kind of story we are when we take time to intentionally rewind our lives. In this exercise, you're helping Millennials identify common themes and patterns based on their defining moments.

While God is the author of our lives, He asks us to co-write our stories with Him. As we turn back the clock and visualize the defining moments in our lives, we can begin to see and understand how God has led us to certain experiences and particular people who have helped shape us into who we are today.

1. Journal eight to ten defining moments that have shaped who you are today—both positive and negative experiences in your life. What are some big wins and accomplishments? What about seasons of trial and failures? Think through illustrations drawn from various periods in your life, such as elementary school, junior high, high school, college and post-college.

2. Draw a horizontal line on a blank piece of paper. Mark above or below the horizontal line depending on how positive or negative each experience was. Be concrete with what happened. For positive experiences, draw a line on the top; for negative experiences, draw them below.

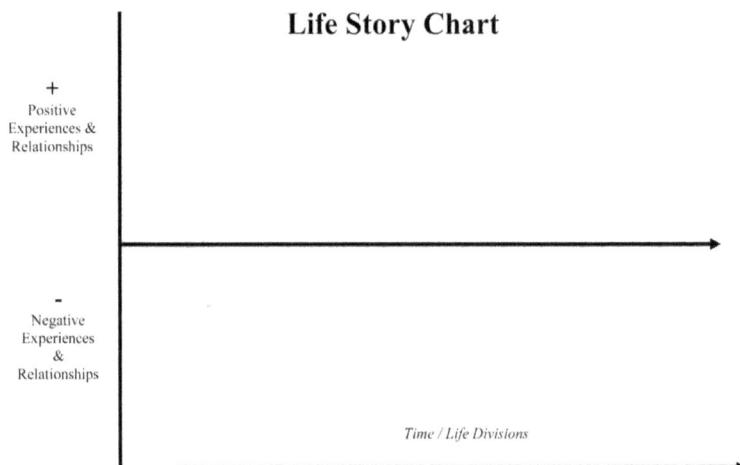

Life Story Chart

+
Positive
Experiences &
Relationships

-
Negative
Experiences
&
Relationships

Time / Life Divisions

3. Pay attention to the verbs you're using to describe these defining moments. These verbs are hints to help you discover prominent themes or patterns that emerge out of your story. Think about pivotal people in those experiences. What can you know about your wiring and tendencies? For the negative experiences, what did you learn from them?

4. Reveal your timeline and story with your friend, family, mentor, or trusted inner circle. Share the details of your story. Ask them for feedback on how they have played a role in your upbringing. What recurring themes do you notice? Is there anything missing from this story that you overlooked?

Going through this exercise helps you see what it's really like to be on the other side of you. It reveals your personality, talent and passions. It opens and closes doors—shaping a beautiful narrative that God is writing in your life.

Note: This process might require Millennials to muster the courage to confront and surface painful memories they've kept hidden and even pushed back into the recesses of their mind. It's not easy. Encourage them to ask for encouragement and prayer as they seek to gain greater clarity around who they are and how God has shaped their story.

It is in our story that we discover our calling.

ENDNOTES

1. https://www.buxtonco.com/blog/targeting-millennials-with-customer-analytics

2. Ibid.

3. *Quarter-Life Calling* by Paul Sohn, FaithWords; Exp Rev edition (April 4, 2017).

4. *The Call* by Os Guinness, Thomas Nelson, 2003.

5. *More* by Todd Wilson, Zondervan, 2016.

6. Ibid.

7. Ibid.

8. *Courage and Calling* by Gordon Smith, IVP, 2011.

9. Barna Research, https://www.barna.com/research/americans-divided-on-the-importance-of-church/#.UzwMlq1dW7o

10. *Souls in Transition* by Christian Smith and Patricia Snell, Oxford University Press, 2009.

11. https://factsandtrends.net/2014/05/16/6-reasons-millennials-arent-at-your-church/

12. *Souls in Transition* by Christian Smith and Patricia Snell, Oxford University Press, 2009.

13. http://www.lifelongfaith.com/uploads/5/1/6/4/5164069/family_faith_formation.pdf

14. https://www.barna.com/research/what-millennials-want-when-they-visit-church/

15. http://www.faithformationlearningexchange.net/uploads/5/2/4/6/5246709/best_practices_in_family_faith_formation.pdf

16. *The Millennials* by Thom S. Rainer and Jess W. Rainer, B&H Books, 2011.

17. *Generational IQ* by Haydn Shaw, Tyndale Momentum. 2015.

18. https://www.cnbc.com/2018/06/20/millennials-moving-out-of-mom-and-dads-place-study-shows.html

19. McCann Worldgroup, a leading global marketing services company, reports that half of Millennials would give up their sense of smell to keep their computer or mobile phones.

20. https://www.barna.com/research/americans-divided-on-the-importance-of-church/#.V-hxhLVy6FD

21. https://www.thegospelcoalition.org/article/ministering-to-millennials-in-a-secular-age

22. http://www.pewsocialtrends.org/2010/02/24/millennials-confident-connected-open-to-change/

23. *You Lost Me* by David Kinnaman, Baker Books, 2016.

24. Ibid.

25. https://www.barna.com/research/5-reasons-millennials-stay-connected-to-church/#.UjrqWMZJNVK

26. *You Lost Me* by David Kinnaman, Baker Books, 2016.

27. Ibid.

28. "Who You Say I Am," Hillsong Worship.

29. *The Call* by Os Guinness, Thomas Nelson, 2003.

30. *Without Rival* by Lisa Bevere, Revell, 2016.

31. https://www.firstthings.com/web-exclusives/2016/10/the-priesthood-of-all-believers

32. *Hero Maker* by Dave Ferguson and Warren Bird, Zondervan, 2018.

33. https://positiveorgs.bus.umich.edu/news/teaching-the-reflected-best-self-exercise-for-personal-development/

34. *Good to Great* by Jim Collins, HarperBusiness, 2001.

ABOUT THE AUTHORS

Paul Sohn is a leadership coach, best-selling author and speaker. Formerly employed by both a Fortune 50 company and a Top 100 Great Place to Work Company, Paul is the founder of QARA.

He is also the best-selling author of ***Quarter-Life Calling: Pursuing Your God-Given Purpose in Your Twenties*** and has been named one of the "Top 33 under 33 Christian Millennials to Follow" by *Christianity Today*.

In 2016, Paul received the John C. Maxwell Transformational Leadership Award. Some of his favorite things include authentic Korean food, tennis, and traveling. Paul currently resides in Orange County, California.

Derek Bell launched Mosaic Strategy Group in 2005 and was promptly commissioned by Bob Buford with launching The Drucker Institute in Claremont, California (you can read that story in *Drucker & Me* by Bob Buford).

Since that time, Derek has had the great privilege of working with a myriad of global thought leaders on issues important to the church and society while also serving in leadership positions in two Nashville, Tennessee, area churches.

In addition to leading the Mosaic Strategy Group (www.mosaicstrategy.us), Derek currently serves as the executive director of Made for More (www.personalcalling.org), a daughter ministry of Exponential, as well as The Buford Library (www.bufordlibrary.org). Both organizations are working to transform the latent energy in Christ followers into active energy. Derek is passionate about helping every disciple of Christ discover, engage and walk in the unique calling God has for them.

Together with his wife, Jennifer, they have the great privilege of being Mom and Dad to Macy, Parker and Grayson. As a family, the Bells are involved in caring for orphans and widows through the non-profit Both Hands, where Derek serves as chairman of the board. The Bell family lives in Brentwood, Tennessee.

QUARTER-LIFE CALLING

PURSUING YOUR GOD-GIVEN PURPOSE IN YOUR TWENTIES

"Every person who's young or young at heart
needs to read this...and this is a book that
will guide you out of that confusion and into
the clarity that is your calling."

· JEFF GOINS
BESTSELLING AUTHOR OF "THE ART OF WORK"

"This is a book for millennials who want
to break free from the rat race–for those
who believe they were created for something
more."

BRAD LOMENICK
FORMER PRESIDENT OF CATALYST AND AUTHOR OF
H3 LEADERSHIP

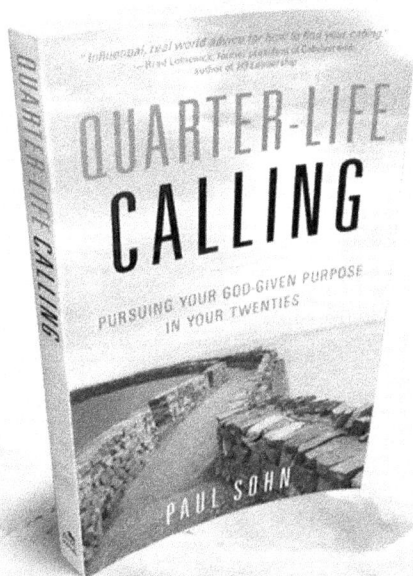

In Quarter-Life Calling, best-selling
author Paul Sohn shares practical
insights around how to discover your
calling in your emerging adulthood.
Even though he seemed to have
achieved it all, including landing his
dream job at a Fortune 500 company,
throughout his twenties Paul Sohn
struggled with feelings of inadequacy,
emptiness, and disillusionment. This
book will help you turn your "quarter-
life crisis" into a season of finding
your quarter-life calling.

QARA